A Mississippi Girl Remembers

by
Mildred Price Smith

Copyright 2008 by the author, Mildred Price Smith

Fortuity Press – Publisher
Astor, Florida USA
www.fortuitypress.com

All rights reserved. Reproduction in whole or in part is prohibited without prior written permission from the publisher.

Printed in the United States of America

Table of Contents

Preface   iii

Acknowledgements   iv

Chapter 1: In the Beginning …The Family   1

Chapter 2: A Kid on a Farm   14

Chapter 3: Nursing … My Calling   30

Chapter 4: We're In the Army Now   38

Chapter 5: A Second Calling   69

Epilogue   74

Map of Germany   75

Appendix: Assorted Photos   76

Preface:

Looking back at one's life gives the one looking and their family a sense of place in the family heritage. From such recollections we learn about simple and profound events that dramatically affected our lives and that continue to....

These things bind us together and give us insight into our family history and its legacy... we must all pass this history on and write our own.

As each life progresses it blends with others creating a unified whole that connects us all.

Write your own story and pass it on and encourage others to as well.

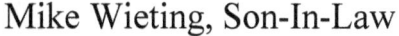

Mike Wieting, Son-In-Law

Acknowledgements:

My heartfelt thanks to my niece, Janet Laws, who lives in Price, Utah. She typed and retyped, while giving me pointers on what I should say to be more clear. Her help was absolutely crucial.

My sincere thanks to daughter, Shelley and husband Dr. Mike, for providing so many things that I could never have done, like putting this book together, and inserting the photos correctly. Also thanks to Linda Keilman for her assistance in formatting the text and making this look more polished.

Photo taken at Matty Hersee, early 40's

Chapter 1
In the Beginning ... The Family

My grandfather was primarily a farmer, but he also was skilled in sharpening the grist mill which ground corn into corn meal. When he could no longer farm, two of his sons, (one of them being my Papa,) bought part of his father's land. Papa had a total of 320 acres, lots of land on which to raise a family and his crops.

At the age of two and a half, Papa had polio. The result was that his one leg and foot did not develop properly, making him walk on the side of that foot. You didn't notice it much because he could do everything on the farm but plow; he couldn't keep up with the horse. He was a very strong man. I remember him lying on the floor with three of us small children standing on his chest. Later in his life he had to walk with a cane or a walker.

I was told that when Papa was young you did not dare him to do anything. One day while he was using a hammer, Aunt Lillie, his sister, walked up and impudently said, "I bet you can't make me move my toe." Well, she moved it, and never did that again!

When Papa was a boy, there was no rural mail delivery. The closest town was Quitman, the county seat of Clarke County. When his father worked away from home, Grandma would send Papa, even as early as nine years of age, to town in a wagon, similar to buckboards seen in western movies, to pick up the mail. He apparently showed that he could be depended on at an early age; he remained a very dependable person throughout his life. He would do what any other young boy would do, just hang around town and see what was going on. Papa loved going to town as long as he lived; he would stay there all day.

A handsome, young Bailey Price

Bailey Price, atop a load of log, date of photo unknown

I was born on a farm in Clarke County Mississippi, one of nine children. Our parents, Bailey and Nella Price, were very caring, Godly people.

The most important thing about my Dad was doing things well, and teaching his kids to do the same. He was wise beyond his years. He ran a grist mill, grinding corn into meal for people in our community and for miles around. I was very small the first time I remember visiting Papa while grinding corn into meal. I never saw the rocks inside, but remember that the shelled corn was put into the mill (taken off the cob.) One setting would cause the corn to be ground into meal, and another setting would grind the corn into bigger pieces, which we called "chops." That was used mostly for chicken feed. Papa had a set of sharp metal picks on the end of a handle about the size of a hammer handle. He would use these picks to make very sharp places on the rocks, which would cause the corn to come out very fine, in other words, as meal, or if less sharp, would make the corn into "chops". Papa's pay for grinding corn was a certain amount of the meal.

When he had a mill-sharpening job Papa would go by horseback or buggy and stayed in the home of someone on the route, probably the person whose mill he was working on. He was usually away no more than two or three days at a time. He would put four or five of the picks in a bag and either hang it on the saddle or put them in the buggy.

Papa liked the buggy because it had springs, making it a much smoother ride. He also had a Model T Ford; he said you could go anywhere in it, but usually had to spend some money on it before you got home.

Papa also operated a steam syrup mill. We did not grow the sugar cane; we got it from other farmers who cut down the cane stalks and brought them to us. Papa ran the syrup mill that ground the juice out of the cane by pressing the stalks. He had a huge machine called an evaporator with pipes in the bottom that was operated by steam. He would empty a number of barrels of juice into the evaporator and it cooked over the steam filled pipes. He could cook 36 gallons of ribbon syrup in one cooking. Papa had a knack for knowing just when it was ready to drain from the evaporator into the gallon cans. We used this same syrup to pull taffy candy. I shall never forget the taste of cold sugar cane juice on an October or November morning.

I remember he loved people, and interacting with strangers. He would be the first to greet someone and tell him his name. Everyone knew him.

Mama said she actually cut wood for wood stoves when she was only twelve years old. When she was 19 she came to live with her father in the same community where Papa lived. Because most preachers had several churches to go to every Sunday, the little country Methodist church Grandpa Redden attended had an afternoon service. Mama and Grandpa Redden came one Sunday afternoon and that's where she met Papa. He was with another girl and for awhile he would see one girl on one Sunday and the other girl the next Sunday. But Mama said it wasn't long before he saw only her. I think it was in April that they set their wedding day for July 14, 1910.

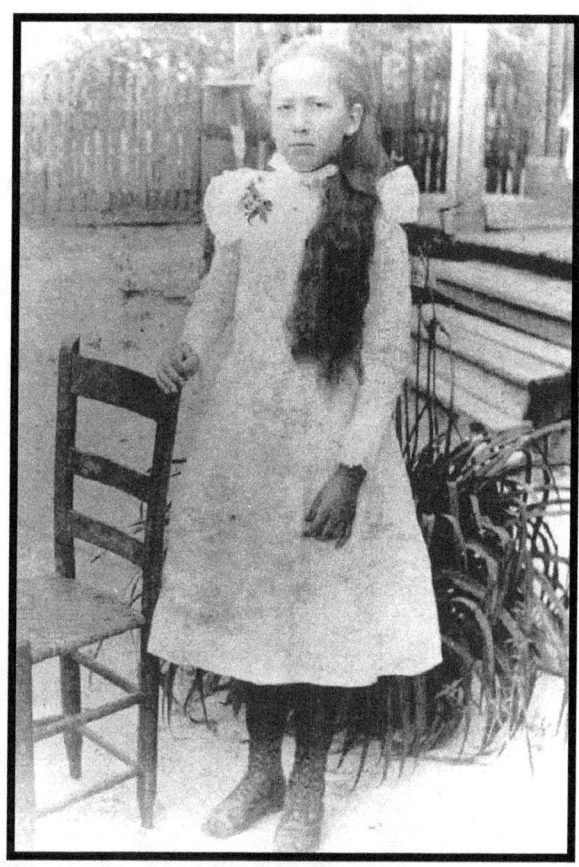

My mother, Nella Redden at age 10

Today we would probably call Mama a recycler. She re-used everything. Family members would bring her scraps of fabric from new dress material and she made beautiful quilts with them. She raised watermelons and garden vegetables and kept the seeds to plant the next year.

Mama was born and reared in Alabama. Her mother died when she was only eight days old, possibly from blood loss following the delivery. There were no medications available that could stop the bleeding. Mama had one brother, two half sisters and a half brother. She was taken from Alabama and reared by her grandmother who was 52 when she took over the task. They were very poor; they had a piece of leased or rented land and sold eggs, chickens, and butter, if they had a cow. Mama also worked on other farms picking cotton, hoeing corn, doing whatever, for pay. They had a little house and garden.

The young Price family: From far right, Bailey and Nella Price with Kathleen on her lap. Also in photo: Grandpa Price with Aunt Lillie in center, Lillie's husband Bob (not shown) was a Methodist preacher in Louisiana. Far left is Papa's brother, Uncle Doug and Aunt Charlie with their first four children, Joe, Millicent, Brogan and George.

There were nine of us children; six girls and three boys. The youngest, my sister Joan, died in 1940. When she was eleven years old her school teacher sent word to my parents that Joan was having trouble seeing the black board. After examining her, the local eye doctor said he thought her eye problem was being caused from another area of her body. A test on her kidneys revealed that they were affected. The doctor began treating her with medications. The next time she was scheduled to see the doctor, Joan and Mama met Aunt Lillian for lunch. After lunch Joan took a nap…but did not wake up. She was admitted to the hospital, but Joan lived only one week. She died the week I graduated from high school. Post mortems were not done much then, so we never really knew what caused her death. One doctor told Lillian that he wished he could have seen inside that child's head.

Me at 5 or 6 yrs old; I started school at 5

*Lucy Mildred Price – High School Graduation Photo
April 1940*

The eldest of my siblings, Kathleen, went to Meridian, Mississippi, after high school to live with Uncle George, my Papa's youngest brother, and took stenography courses. She married Phillip, an insurance adjuster, in 1930. They moved around a bit, like in the military, living in Meridian and Jackson, Mississippi; Nashville and Bristol, Tennessee. They had three daughters; Kathryn, Janis, and Phyllis. Kathryn, the eldest, decided to get involved in her children's school and help kids stay off drugs. She partnered with an off duty police officer and talked to kids at school; even carrying a huge syringe to make the point that no one other than a nurse or doctor should give any type of shot. Janis worked for many years at Coca Cola in Atlanta, and Phyllis has always been very involved with her community and church.

Kathleen cared for all of us, and helped each of us in some way or another; for example supported a niece going to college and put a phone in Mama's house. She loved to travel; in fact, she visited all 48 mainland states in her life. Kathleen was 15 months old when our brother Robert, who she always called Buddy was born. Even after the onset of dementia in later life she would mistakenly call a handy man at her daughter's home "Buddy." Kathleen died on March 4, 2005, at the age of 93, loved and respected by all her family.

The second child, Robert, (Buddy, as we called him) was unique and special. He graduated early from an agricultural high school in 1932, after three years. One year he stayed in the dorm and to pay his tuition, milked cows for our Uncle Raymond who was the teacher. Buddy was married in 1935 to Jessie Beryl Vickers. He met her when she came to Elwood to teach elementary school. Buddy was a very hard-working man, who loved farming and just seeing things grow. He farmed his own land and leased more, all the land he could find that wasn't in use, so that he could plant more. Buddy grew mostly edible things, like corn, peas, and other vegetables. He especially enjoyed growing watermelons and was very good at it. Once a friend from Quitman came to see me in El Paso, Texas, and brought me a huge watermelon, 23 inches long; from Buddy. He sold things to the people in the community and once filled an eighteen wheeler with watermelons for shipment up north.

Buddy was like the Pied Piper; grandchildren followed him around and many youth in the community helped in his fields. He taught many of them to drive, even though some were only ten or eleven years old. He would tell them, "Try second, that's a mighty good gear." My son, Bryan, was one of those young drivers; in fact he ran over a section of his Uncle Buddy's new fence. Buddy didn't even get upset.... he was a very patient man. Buddy worked for and also retired from the railroad, but he was a farmer all his life. Jessie taught for 25 years in Quitman Elementary school. He and his wife had two children; Beryl, a high school history teacher, and Bob, a pastor in California, whose first career was as a civil service aeronautical engineer. Buddy died March 30, 1995 and Jessie, the following year in August, 1996. Even at Buddy's funeral, the preacher referred to him as "the vegetable man".

After Buddy came Mary, who with her husband Lester, had three girls and one son. She spent her life in and around Clarke County, and provided child care for individuals, besides raising her own. She was a good care giver, even after she ended up in a nursing home, she would help take care of the other residents. She and her husband separated and she lived for quite a while with our mother, in the family home. Hers was not a happy life and she struggled with depression at times. Her eldest daughter, Mary Elessie, said to be the smartest girl who ever graduated from Quitman High School, works in a psychiatric hospital as a social worker. The second daughter, Shelia, is a registered nurse and lives in Barnett ,Ms. The third daughter, Diane, lives in Bessemer, Alabama, and the son, Leroy, lives in Shubuta, Ms. Mary died on January 1, 1994, at the age of 79.

Lillian was the next child. She became a registered nurse in 1936, having trained in Meridian, at Anderson's Hospital. She worked many years as a supervisor at Anderson's and retired from there. In 1938 she married Gus Ward, who worked at the post office, and they had five children. Two of her daughters, Martina and Carol, are teachers; two sons, Bill and Albert, are in business; and another daughter, Aurelia, is a registered nurse. Lillian currently lives in an independent living apartment community in Meridian, Ms. and spends much of her time with family activities.

My brother John was the child just older than me. He and I were close all our lives. I was too small to remember this, but Mama told me many times that I would be outside playing with John, but if I cried, she didn't have to worry because she knew John would bring me to safety…from a horse, a cow, or the model T Ford. He always took care of me. John was working a pipeline job when he was drafted into the Army. He was sent overseas in World War II for 30 months and served mostly in North Africa and Italy. He returned home in the summer of 1945, with a diagnosis of schizophrenia. He married Lona Freeman on September 7 of that year, the same night my husband and I got married. He had four daughters; Gloria, June, Nella, and Linda. As John's mental illness progressed, he was committed to a VA psychiatric facility in October 1958. He spent most of the rest of his life in and out of VA facilities. He came to visit Mama a few times but if he failed to take his medications he had to go back to the facility. John, often in conflict with the hospital staff, didn't think he needed medication, so there was constant turmoil from 1958 until he died in 2002. His daughter Linda and I made many trips to Alabama to visit him after I came home to live in 1993. I would do his nails and Linda usually fed him lunch.

Parkinson's disease prevented him from using his hands. Our younger brother, James, was his executor and was able, through people he knew, to invest enough of John's money so there was enough for John's family after his death. John died of pneumonia on August 16, 2002.

James came after me, known by the family as Doug. When he joined the Air Force in 1942 it was said about him that he was one of the best pilots the Air Force had. He flew in World War II, Korea, and Viet Nam. James met his wife, Maybelle, while in the military at San Marcos, Texas. Maybelle, also serving in the military, was from Pine Bluff, Arkansas. They were married for 58 years and had three sons, Jimmy, Gerry, and Tommy, and one daughter, Sue. Jimmy, the oldest, retired as a park ranger; Gerry became a lab tech after serving as an interpreter in the military, Tommy drives a school bus while studying to be a history teacher, and Sue, still living on the family farm, works in the local library and raises dogs. Gerry died on Feb.2, 2005 after a battle with cancer. James retired from the military at the rank of Lt. Colonel. Later, he was elected to the Mississippi House of Representatives and served for twelve years. He was found to have lung cancer in the late '90's and died on October 8, 2002. One of James' grandsons followed his lead by graduating from the Air Force Academy and becoming a pilot. He is now on active duty serving at the rank of Lt. Colonel.

The youngest of my surviving siblings is Ruth. She also became a registered nurse, having trained in Meridian, at Rush Hospital. Meridian had three hospitals, each with its own training school for nurses. Ruth and her husband, Maurice, married for 53 years, had two daughters; Evelyn, a registered nurse, and Joann, a teacher; and two sons; Mark, who works in clothing sales, and Malcolm, an attorney. Ruth and Maurice also opened their home to two pre-teen girls whose mother was terminally ill with cancer. She asked them to take her children just prior to her death. They did, and the girls, Betty and Sonny, were as loyal to the family as if they had been blood relatives. Both are married and have children of their own. Maurice is now deceased.

My father, Bailey Price, early 1900's

Chapter 2
A Kid on a Farm

With so many nurses in the family, I am reminded of health care on the farm. For the most part, it was non-existent, especially for childhood diseases like whooping cough, mumps, chicken pox, measles, and flu. More care was taken when the whole family had the measles. We all had to stay in the dark because it was believed that exposure to light might permanently affect our eyes. Buddy was 15 years old when he caught the measles and brought it home to the rest of us. Since he recovered first, he helped nurse the rest of us. He served us "sweet water," a mixture of water and syrup. It seemed that every time I looked up Buddy was filling our glasses. We didn't know it then, but forced fluids were actually good for us. I was very small when all of us got whooping cough. I had to be picked up every time I coughed. Mama had six children with the cough at the same time.

Around a farm there can be many boards with nails, usually rusty ones with plenty of bacteria. Our treatment for getting one of these nails in your foot was to sit down and put your foot into a pan filled with kerosene oil (also used to fuel our lamps, since there was no electricity in the farm house until I was in high school in the 1930's.) We would soak the injured foot for 30 minutes, three times a day. This must have been a great treatment as none of us ever developed tetanus. Today you just get a tetanus shot.

Mama's father, Grandpa Redden, outlived three wives. He did some farming, but after the last wife died, he gave up the farm and began spending three weeks with each of his five children. When the three weeks was up he would put his hat on his head and sit all day waiting for his son, Uncle Raymond, to pick him up. To have Grandpa Redden at our house for three weeks was a joyful time. He would tell us stories at the supper table. Once he told us of a woman who had a hard time getting along. My sister Ruth was listening so intently that she asked him, "Is she getting along okay now?" He had a big laugh over that. Once he was hunting for his pipe and it was in the corner of his mouth the whole time! We all had a good laugh at that one. He died at the age of 87 and was buried near my childhood home.

I began school at the age of five. I remember when I was just learning to whistle. I practiced my new skill one day in class at school and promptly received a whipping. We walked two miles every day to our little two-teacher country school house. It had only two classrooms, but it did have a small auditorium with a stage where we had plays. Our elementary school consisted of grades one through eight. My favorite teacher was Miss Riley, who taught me in the 2nd, 3rd, and 4th grades. She did special things like decorating the blackboard, drawing an old tree with partially broken limbs, putting a squirrel on each end of it, and drawing green grass with lots of flowers in between. She did this with pastel chalk, which we had never seen before. She also had a unique way of teaching multiplication tables. She would draw a big circle on the black board with numbers 1 through 12, like a clock. She placed a number in the center then skipped around, pointing to the numbers on the edge of the circle. We were to multiply that number by the one in the center in our heads and give her the answer. Because of this drill for the 4th graders, all four of us, we knew those multiplication tables so well that she could not stump us. I'm the only one from that class still living.

Our favorite game at elementary school was town ball. It was played like baseball except there was no one on the bases. We "got them out" by cutting them off between bases, catching a fly, or striking out. There was lots of "noise" about whether someone was out or not, but we were really friends.

First row left to right: James D. Price, Eula Neal Jacobs, Hazel Davis, Opal Mason, Ruth Brown. Second row: John Holloman, Jr., Annie Bell Nichols, Fred Burt, O. C. Evans, Rufus Sinclair, or Martin Sinclair, Mary Ellen Boykin, Mildred Price. Third row: Chester Evans, ?, Eugine Davis, ?, Dan McGowan, ?, Ruth Burt, Eula Burt, Oberia Burt. Back (center) Mrs. Izzie Riley Volking, teacher.

A group shot of my class at school, four grades

In all I had eight years of elementary school and four years of high school. Courses in high school included four years of English, math, algebra, geometry, history, one semester of Latin…the usual. I wasn't a great student, but I received passing grades.

I think it was in the summer of my 10th year that I had the chance to travel with a favorite aunt to visit her sister. When I left home I had 22 sores on one leg between my knee and ankle. Aunt Charlie had me take a concoction which she had mixed. Every day I took one teaspoon full with lots of water from the pump outside. I don't remember just how long I stayed with her, but when I went home I had no more sores. She later told me what I had been taking. It was parched, crushed egg shells mixed with cream of tartar. She didn't tell me at the time because she was afraid I'd refuse to drink it.

Also, around the age of 10, I was taken to the charity hospital by my uncle, my dad's youngest brother, to have my tonsils removed. I was in the hospital two nights, and then I stayed with my uncle and aunt. They had three daughters, and one of them sewed very well. They gave me a beautiful doll and their daughter, my cousin, made me 18 dresses for her. Can you imagine...a country girl with a doll and 18 dresses! I was on cloud nine. Unfortunately I didn't have the doll very long. One of my brothers pulled the head off the same day I came home from the hospital. Even back then in the 1930's brothers could be a pain.

My high school was five miles from home, so we got to ride the bus which came by our house. My friend and I had a favorite game at school...we pitched washers. (round discs of metal with a hole in the center) To play, we dug a small hole in the ground, a little larger than the washer. Points were earned in the following manner: one in the hole counted three points and right on the edge counted one point; the game went to 21 points. Two people played at once. The holes were dug about ten feet apart. We were the school champs. We ate our lunch, which we brought from home, as fast as we could, then went out and played; everyone who came along, and we beat them all.

Home economics was quite interesting. I remember that it was 90 minutes long. One day one of the girls at my table was having a birthday. There was plenty of time during class for me to read the recipe, bake and ice a chocolate cake, and for all of us to eat it before the period ended. We learned about primary and secondary colors, architecture, cooking and sewing. During the year we each had to make at least one new piece of clothing for ourselves. We then had a fashion show, complete with high heels to show off our handiwork.

On our farm we raised all kinds of things; garden vegetables, corn, potatoes, and watermelons. We had a pear tree and we picked wild blackberries for canning and making pies in the winter. We didn't have to buy much, mostly things like coffee, tea, sugar, flour, rice, etc., We bought these items on credit until fall when we sold cotton, our money crop. Cotton was so important that the start of school would be delayed if it was ready to pick. [Cotton locks are five separate pieces of fluffy, white cotton hanging out of a boll.] We took a sack with a strap attached to it which we put over our shoulder, then dragged the sack along the row as we pulled the cotton from the boll and put it in the sack. I could only pick about 79 pounds of cotton a day. When you picked for another farmer, you were paid so much for 100 pounds. Sometimes we had other people picking with us. Since my Papa had polio, he had Mama make him some knee pads so that he could pick the cotton on his knees. He did this all day long. He was the hardest working man I've ever known. When you have a disabled father work all day on his knees, you try your hardest to be the best you can.

Taking the cotton to a gin was an interesting activity. All the seeds were removed by the machinery of the gin and then the beautiful clean white cotton was packed into a burlap wrapper and strapped so it couldn't fall out. We called that finished product a bale: these usually weighed 500 to 600 pounds each. Papa also did gin reporting: compiling the amounts of cotton ginned at each of the cotton gins in the area, which was tracked by the state.

My father loved hatching and caring for baby chicks. We raised as many as the incubator would hold: I think it held about 200 eggs. It had a large tray and was fired by a kerosene lamp on the side. The best temperature for developing chicks is 103 degrees. We would put a mark on one side of each egg and then every night and morning we turned the eggs, just like a mother hen does. After three weeks the chicks began to crack the shells. We loved watching through the glass window in the door to the incubator for the chicks to break their shells. We were told never to help a chick break out because if it wasn't strong enough to get out by itself, it probably would be crippled and might not live.

Left to Right: Mary (standing), Papa (on his knees), John, Doug, Mildred, and Lillian. This field was called the long row patch, the longer the rows, the more cotton produced.

We raised lots of peanuts. We grew so many that it would take four of us all day long to plant them. We would drop the seeds one at a time about a foot apart in a shallow row, then someone would follow with a light plow and cover them up. Peanuts grow underground in a root system in sandy soil. We pulled them up at harvest and allowed them to lay there until dry. Then we hauled them to the barn in a wagon and put them in the loft. All through the winter we picked the peanuts off the roots. The plants or vines we put down in the hay rack in the mule stable were to be used for feed. During the winter we roasted lots of peanuts and then made peanut candy with the sugar cane syrup Papa made. It was delicious and so good for you!

There were always chores when we came home from school; things like picking vegetables, sometimes cotton, feeding the animals, or gathering eggs. As soon as we got home, we would get a big baked pear or sweet potato, and then go right to work. My brothers hunted and killed squirrels and rabbits, which we ate. We did our home work after supper by the light of an oil lamp on the kitchen table.

There were plenty of chores, but there were fun times, also. The ole swimming hole was a good sized creek of running water. My brothers would take a large hook, several inches long, and put a little minnow on the hook then leave it over night. The next morning they would check their catch. Once they had an eleven-pound catfish on the hook. We loved to play in the creek. We were so noisy; we ran the black and green water moccasin snakes out of our swimming hole, which went upstream and never came back.

On the farm, the 4th of July was always a very special day. We usually had relatives visiting. We always had fried chicken and home-made ice cream. You haven't experienced country life until you've sat on a burlap bag on top of a freezer while someone turns the crank until the custard freezes.

Another fun thing was pulling taffy. We cooked a small amount of cane syrup in the boiler on top of the stove. We tested the syrup to see if we could make a firm ball in cold water. Then we poured the syrup on a butter-greased plate. When it was cool enough, we buttered our very clean hands, took the syrup in our hands and pulled it back and forth. It went from a red color to yellow. Then we cut it with scissors into little pillow-like shapes.

Easter was another special time. We always had an Easter egg hunt and the neighbor kids came. Mama and my special Aunt Charlie hid the eggs in the woods above our house. They always put one in a tree so we would race to see who got it. After finding all the eggs we could, Mama would have us line up and show how many eggs each of us had found. She knew how many they had hidden, so she went with a stick and poked around until she found them all.

Christmas was a quiet holiday for us. We did not have a tree; we could have had one, but they weren't much in vogue then. We hung our stockings in our parent's bedroom where there was a huge fireplace. I always had a doll in my stocking. Other gifts back in the 20's and 30's were apples, oranges, huge raisins, Brazil nuts, and firecrackers. Once one of my brothers threw a lit firecracker under our bed...that really woke us up! My dad liked to take a whole string of the little firecrackers and light them in the street of Quitman.

There are many sounds at night in the country. We slept with our windows open so we heard them all night long. As a young person, my favorites were the song of a whip-o-will and the sound of a lonesome train far away. But, we also heard crickets and the frogs which lived in our ponds; they do a lot of croaking especially after a good rain.

My family's first house burned down. It had been built by my father and a carpenter. One day Papa was writing a list of things he was to buy in town. He tossed a piece of paper he didn't need into the fireplace, before he left for town. The wind carried that little piece of paper up the chimney and onto the roof which was quite high; the house was supposed to be two stories. After smoldering a while, it eventually caught fire. When they first realized the house was on fire, the only other adult there besides Mama, an elderly farm worker, tried to extinguish the fire by throwing dippers of water at the flame.

The roof was quite steep. Mama had a terrible time trying to save some things while keeping up with her kids. The adult was there to fill the wood box on her stove, as she only had a fireplace and wood burning stove. Mama tried to take some things out of the house, but she didn't realize she was putting them too close to the fire. So she lost some of them, also. Papa didn't know the house had burned down until he came home from town 5 miles away, in the wagon.

Eighteen months passed after the house burned before a new one was built. In the interim, the family lived in a 3 room, potato house. This building had two concrete floored rooms and the third room was a shop for working on tools for farming. Normally, this was where we stored the sweet potatoes in the fall and winter. You put them in hay so they don't rot as easily. It was little more than a shed, but Mama said it was the coolest place she ever lived.

A very old photo of the old home, prior to the fire

My brother John was a baby when the house burned, but by the time the new one was built, he was big enough to help a bit. Mama told us he carried the coffee pot into the new house. That was in April, before I was born on August 21, 1921.

Our second home was a big, six-room house. All of the siding came from one Cypress tree. It had three bedrooms, a kitchen, living and dining rooms, a long hall and two porches. Our heat was from a wood stove and a fireplace. Three girls slept in each adult-size bed and wore flannel pajamas or gowns. Just before going to our cold bedroom, we washed our feet in hot water, and then ran down the hall to our beds. Since Mama made her own quilts; we had so much cover we could hardly turn over. To this day I don't heat my house at night. The girls' room had two double beds and so did the boys room as well as the one in my parent's room; this meant we needed a lot of quilts. My mother received scraps of material from family members and others to make the quilt tops. Once I remember, she decided to buy red bandana handkerchiefs and made the entire quilt top by sewing those together. Her quilting frame was made with four pieces of lumber, tied together and suspended from the ceiling. She would lower the frame when she was ready to work on the current quilt. One day my sister Mary took a match from the mantle and without thinking struck it on the side of the quilt frame. Since the lining was flannel, it burst into flames and my sisters and I had to literally pull the whole quilt out of the frame so we wouldn't set the house on fire. That was the end of the bandana quilt.

Mama and Papa Price with a guest on the front porch of the house built after the fire

The old house is still standing. However, it's in bad shape now... due to termites. I lived there from the day I was born until I left home in 1941 to study nursing. A niece now lives there and runs a kennel and raises a number of breeds, including Great Danes, on the property.

I appreciate the encouragement I received from my parents and teachers, especially my elementary teachers. My Bible teachers in Sunday school helped instill in me the knowledge of right and wrong. Our parents taught us to obey them, our teachers, and all older people. We also learned that we didn't call older people by their first name.

When we were very young, Mama regularly read a Bible story book to us. Later, of course, we read it for ourselves. We also had "Progressive Farmer" and "Ladies Home Journal." The first whole book I read was *"Gone With The Wind."* I must have been about 20 years old. I remember how much I enjoyed it, and the movie, too.

We went to a small country church which was within walking distance from home, about a mile and a half. It had just a heater for warmth. When I was 17 an elderly gentleman in our community said to me, "Your church needs painting." He belonged to a different church from me. But he said, "I'll give you the first dollar if you ride your horse to visit all the members of your church and collect money for the painting." I did and I collected $57. I guess we painted the church…at this point it's not clear whether we did or not. On Sunday we always attended Sunday school and church. Since this was way before television, and we did not have electricity for a radio, our music was mostly hymns that we learned in church.

I remember having only one dog on the farm. Her name was Bessie. She was half bull dog and was so much fun. We sat on the front porch on Sundays after church and lunch, and Bessie would be with us. Papa could say in a very ordinary tone of voice, "Bessie, go get the mules." She would immediately get up, go to the pasture, and bark until all the mules were standing at the back gate to the barn. Two of my brothers liked to pitch a ball back and forth; Bessie would often get between them and catch the ball in her mouth.

In this farming community we were all pretty much friends. I remember once Papa allowed several of us siblings to attend a neighborhood party a little over two miles away. We put chairs in the back of our wagon and off we went. When we got to the party, we tied the mules to a tree out front of the house. It wasn't long before the noise of the party scared the mules into breaking loose and heading for home. Of course we left also, picking up cane-bottom chairs en route. When we arrived home, there were the mules, standing at the barn gate. It was a revolting development...walking over two miles carrying our chairs.

Saturdays were the days for cleaning the house, raking yards, washing clothes and hair. Washing clothes was a production back then because you had to heat the water in large pots outside and then wash the clothes in an old wringer machine. This was long before dryers were available so all the clean clothes were hung outside to dry.

Summers in Mississippi are very hot and humid. We would sit on the porch after supper, hoping our beds would get cool. One exercise we did was for each of us to pick a song and sing it, trying to see how long we could remember the words and music. We sang songs like "She'll Be Coming 'Round the Mountain," "Old McDonald Had a Farm," and "Clementine."

There wasn't a great deal of criticism of the government or the President back then. My father called the government "Uncle Sam." I think he thought that they were doing a good job for the country.

The worst experience of my life was seeing a man shoot his pregnant wife to death. This man rented a house from my father. His wife had left him so he hung around their house all day. Late in the afternoon, the wife and her twin sister came back to the house Papa owned. The man had borrowed a gun while she was away. He went into the house, got the gun and began scaring the girls. My father asked him to bring the gun to him, but about half way to our house, he told the sister to get out of the way, and he shot his wife. I was just a few yards away. As soon as he shot her, I ran into our house. The man ran past our barn, kicked off his shoes, went up to the highway and hid under a bridge. He was found and arrested that same day. He was put into the penitentiary where he spent the rest of his life. Her family told me that he was a jealous man. I remember I didn't sleep that night.

Mama was a great one for helping others. Back then, we sat up with the sick or the dead in their homes. She bathed five of a neighbor's eight children at birth. But she was always home when we came home from school. She had so many talents. She kept a clean house. She was a fantastic cook and loved to cook for family members. She always seemed to have her whole meal ready to serve at one time, regardless of how many dishes were involved. Later when our family grew to be a big crowd, the adults ate in the dining room and the grandchildren ate at the table in the kitchen. That table seated at least 14. As long as I lived at home, and later when I returned for a visit, I preferred to eat with the children in the kitchen. All of Mama's food was good, but I remember the fried chicken, rice and chicken gravy was best of all. The source of the chicken was right outside in the chicken yard. I know there were times, and family enough, that we killed and cooked six frying-sized chickens for one meal.

I lived in the same farm house in which I was born in 1921, until I left home in 1941 to study nursing. On the left side of the house looking from the back, Mama always had a big garden. You could drive from the road to the back door, and then a driveway went around the house opposite the garden to the road in front of the house. Mama had beautiful mimosa trees lining the driveway.

Papa and Mama were married 54 years and one week. Papa's health began deteriorating; high blood pressure and some heart problems. He died in July of 1964 at the age of 83. After Papa died, Mama was very lonely. She did visit me a number of times in El Paso, Texas. She especially liked our Mexican food. In June 1979 during surgery, she was found to have colon cancer. It was too big to remove, and it had already spread so the physicians performed a colostomy, sent her home, and my sisters and I took over her care. One or more of us was with her all the time. She didn't have a lot of pain, in fact, she only had one injection for pain during the whole time. She died on March 22, 1980, just two months short of 89 years old. Family came from all over. My husband and I stayed an extra week, taking dishes back to all those who brought food, and writing thank you notes. When I returned to my home in El Paso, I was moved to write a tribute to my Mama. I sent it to the editor of the El Paso Times and it was published in the Sunday paper on April 6, 1980.

> "I'd like to write a different sort of letter for your column for Easter. You see I've just returned from Mississippi where for the past five weeks I helped care for my 88-year-old mother who had inoperable colon cancer. She passed away in her sleep on March 22.
>
> I wouldn't take a million dollars for that rich experience. She was allowed to stay at home, where she so badly wanted to be, until the end. She loved God and her fellow man and spent her entire life in service to both.
>
> Her care was a family effort, even spilling over to close neighbors. One such man, a neighbor for 46 years who helped lift her the night before she died, remarked that she had bathed five of his nine children at birth.
>
> What we did for Mama is what any family should do who has had so much love and care showered on them all their lives. What makes this an Easter letter was that there is no question where her soul was going. We knew we were

caring for a saint who was soon to receive her just reward.

So I say, go have a great Easter. Rejoice in the true sense, not just with new clothes. It would have been of little significance for Christ to be born and to die...that's what we all do. The good news is that he arose from the dead and offers the same opportunity to us."

Miss Nella Price, the year before her death in 1980

Chapter 3
Nursing ... My Calling

In my last year of high school I had a crush on a young man in the community. He was blue eyed, blonde, and very easy to talk to, but my folks felt I was not ready for marriage. In the 1940's there was not much talk concerning college and there weren't many vocations for girls, especially ones that my family could afford. But there was Mr. Taylor, an elderly gentleman in our community who took a particular interest in me. He encouraged me to stay in school, work hard, and do a good job. Like my mother I have a great desire to help people. When my older sister became a registered nurse, the more I listened and thought about what she had to say, I decided in high school that nursing would be my vocation. I graduated from high school in 1940, and then in June of 1941, four of us from the surrounding communities began training at a charity hospital which had a nurse's training school. Since the hospital was owned and operated by the State of Mississippi, there was no cost for uniforms or books which were furnished to us; of course we had our room, board and laundry. We were paid a few dollars each month all of the three years we were there. We did not enter as a class, just when there was an opening. When we graduated, we became registered nurses after we successfully completed the state board of nursing exams.

Our instruction began almost as soon as we arrived. Everything was so new to me...everything I heard or studied was of great interest. As was common in that day, nursing instruction was in a hospital based program. The patients were on the first two floors, and our dormitories were on the third floor, along with the apartment of the superintendent, who was a physician, appointed by the state. Each time the governor changed, we got a new superintendent. The other medical staff consisted of a surgeon who practiced in Meridian and a house physician who saw patients in a clinic as well as delivering any babies born. There was also an eye doctor who did some cataract surgery. The surgery unit occupied the fourth floor. We had no maids and no aides. There was one day orderly and one night orderly to help with male patients and to mop the floors. The older students taught the new ones. Our learning depended on our assigned patients. For instance, if someone needed an intravenous feeding or a catheter, we learned how to do it at that time.

I showed an aptitude for surgery, so, eight months into my training, I was started in the operating room. We had one house doctor at a time. Since this was a state-run hospital, these positions would change regularly and we had a chance to work with a number of different doctors. I remember all our doctors were kind and helpful. My total time in the OR during the three years I was in training was more than a year. I had the opportunity to teach many other students how to scrub, keep things sterile, and to work closely with the surgeon. Surgery was interesting for many reasons. We learned what the damaged organ we were removing looked like. Also, later, when we were doing similar surgery, we were shown what a healthy one looked like. I knew we were helping people, and that was very important to me.

This photo was probably taken on a Sunday afternoon, during my first year in training at Matty Hersee. We had three hours off each Sunday and often spent time on the lawn.

The Director of Nurses rotated all the students about every five to six weeks. The duties of the surgery team included surgeries, all suture removal, all the deliveries, as well as all fracture care. We made all the things we used; for instance, we made the gauze sponges we used in surgery. We bought large rolls of gauze, cut it into different sizes, folded it so the raw edge would be inside and then sterilized it. We also had powdered glucose with which we made intravenous fluids...so many scoops of powder and water, placed in heavy glass jars and autoclaved to sterilize. We actually had to sharpen the needles used in the intravenous feedings. Many things were not disposable so we had to re-use our supplies...very different from today.

We made plaster of Paris rolls for broken bones by cutting strips of crinoline, placing these on a table on top of each other, rubbing in powdered plaster of Paris until the top one was full, rolling carefully, and placing it in a box until needed. To use these rolls we placed them in warm water until thoroughly wet and then unwrapped them onto the affected limb. We made many at one time because you never knew when they would be used.

Once during my time in training a lady came in from the rural area. She was very much pregnant, so much so that she was x-rayed and found to be carrying triplets. All three were born in good condition, and each weighed over five pounds. She may never have had a prenatal visit; doctors were very scarce in the rural areas. We were all very excited...this was our first and only set of triplets.

Our duty was 10 hours for a day and 12 hours at night. The nurses on night duty would sleep all day, getting up in time for supper at 5:00 p.m. They didn't go on duty until 7:00 p.m. so a favorite pastime was to walk outside along the highway. The hospital was situated where several major highways converged, one going south to a huge Army base called Camp Shelby, and one going west, called Highway 80, to Jackson, our capital city, and further west. World War II began in December 1941 with the bombing of Pearl Harbor in Hawaii and it wasn't long before military convoys, (trucks, jeeps, weapons carriers, etc,) were passing daily. When we walked out near the highway we often found old shell casings, inside of which would be a soldier's address. I wrote to every soldier whose address I found. I remember once at Christmas I had six names and addresses of fellows overseas, one being my brother John's. A local bakery had prepared one-pound fruitcakes with a nice cardboard box to fit. Since I could afford it, I bought six fruitcakes and mailed them to six different theaters of war. The nurses went out with many of the soldiers, and several of these couples married after the war was over.

As part of our training, we had classes from 6:00 to 8:00 p.m., September to May, when our teachers showed up. World War II caused all sorts of shortages, including people to teach the students. Our instructors were a varied lot. A pharmacist taught us medicines, an assortment of doctors came for lectures, one an obstetrician came to help with obstetrics. After spouting off many terms we had never heard before, he closed by asking us, "You understand that?" Then as he left, he said, "It's just like eating lettuce...nothing to it."

The instruction we received depended a lot on who our patients were and what their needs were at the time. Because I had showed an aptitude for surgery, I spent much of my time there and was able to do many things. Although I was not specifically trained to administer anesthesia, I was often asked to do so, under the close supervision of the surgeon. After my training years, I stayed on for an additional year as supervisor of the Operating Room and during that time gave more than sixty patients anesthesia by drop ether.

Another big event of my training was the advent of penicillin. During the war, many of our soldiers developed infected wounds and there was a big interest in solving the problem. One of our doctors showed up at the hospital one day with the first penicillin we had ever seen and I was able to help him mix it and give the first dose we used at Matty Hersee.

I finished my three years of nursing school on July 12, 1944. We did not have a large graduating class because we entered training only a few at a time. I graduated with a close friend who had entered with me. I had hoped to join the Army Nurse Corps because the war was fierce then and nurses were badly needed. However President Roosevelt had had training schools evaluated and ours did not meet the identified criteria. Our evaluation came as a complete surprise. I was told that I'd need supplementary training or I could not join the Corp. I was so upset I wrote to the President. His answer was short – "We're sorry, Miss Price, but we want the very best for our military." Actually we felt that we had a good training school. Recently a doctor said to me, when he learned where I trained, "Oh, you were trained where girls were really taught to be nurses!" My friend and I were asked to stay on at the training school; me as surgery supervisor and she as night supervisor. I was earning some money, enough that I bought gifts and mailed them to my parents for Christmas. One of my favorite treasures is the handwritten thank you letter sent to me by my Papa.

Early in 1945 I read in the <u>Journal of Nursing</u> that Vanderbilt University Hospital had a program to help nurses like me get the additional experience necessary to join the Army Nurse Corps. So I registered and went to Nashville, Tennessee, on June 20, 1945. Nashville was a big city, but I had one purpose for being there. I needed six months training. My supplementary study and duty was on pediatrics, obstetrics and private floor. I had a two-week orientation because I had to learn different ways to chart, even how to make out a charge slip. My training school had been a charity hospital...we never charged for anything.

I rented a room near the hospital. My roommate, Trumy Shaw, was from Ocala, Florida, and she loved to roller skate. She persuaded me to buy some skates. They were the kind that hooked onto your shoes and had to be adjusted with a key. On July 4 she took me to Nashville's beautiful skating rink. It had a lady who played the Hammond organ and a boy who adjusted your skates for you. It was packed with skaters on that national holiday and I was scared. First of all, I did not know how to skate. Second, I had no medical insurance. If I got hurt, I couldn't finish my nursing course. I spent the entire evening holding on to the wall or picking myself up off the floor...that is until I left the floor to have the skate boy adjust my skates. While I was waiting there, I looked up and this handsome, blue-eyed Army Air Force officer asked me to skate with him. I did, for the rest of the evening. I didn't tell him until much later that I was scared and so glad he asked me to skate. He didn't have a car, only a Harley Davidson motorcycle, so I had my first motorcycle ride that night. His name was Robert Smith, and after I met him we were busy. We rode his Harley to parks, the swimming pool, and skating, with our skates slung over the back of the bike. We even rode the Harley to get our marriage license.

That night, July 4, 1945, was the beginning of a whirlwind courtship which culminated in our being married just two months and three days later, on September 7, 1945. Bob had asked me to marry him after only two weeks, and that same night he told me of a girl in Pennsylvania who had been wearing his ring. Fortunately for us, she had just sent it back to him, apparently having determined that their relationship was not to be. Bob asked me if I minded having the same ring reset, and I told him that she couldn't hurt a diamond.(Since that time, the stone has been reset three more times due to wear on the ring, but it is still beautiful.) We were married at the altar of a large Methodist church not far from where I lived. I went to the church and asked the preacher if he would marry us. He agreed and the next Sunday we went to his service. Our marriage was witnessed by my roommate and a Vanderbilt medical student.

Up until that day we went everywhere on the motorcycle. But on our wedding day we bought a little, two-seater coupe automobile. We rented an apartment next to the one I had lived in with my roommate. Bob was stationed 25 miles from Nashville, at a nearby military base. World War II ended on September 2, 1945. In December I successfully finished my supplementary nursing course. Since the war was over and I was just married, I never made it into the Army Nurse Corp. Instead I was appointed as a Red Cross nurse. We were ready to move on.

Robert D. Smith
2nd Lt
Army Air Corps

Photo taken 1943, after graduation from bombardier school in Deming, New Mexico

Bob joined the Army in 1942

Chapter 4
We're In the Army Now

My new husband was a member of the Army Air Corps. During our courtship Bob told me of his wartime experiences. He had been a bombardier on a B-17, flying out of England. In April of 1944 their plane was shot down over Denmark, behind enemy lines. The plane landed in the soft soil of a hay field. All the crew survived, although the co-pilot suffered an injury to his eye. The Danish farmer was there, harrowing his field, and saw that all of the crew got out of the plane. He told them to hide in some woods nearby. This was at 2:00 p.m. They did as they were told, and at 10:00 p.m. the farmer took them to a barn where they were given food and drink and told to sleep in the hay loft. This was the beginning of four days of hiding and moving under cover of darkness. One night they were housed in the apartment of an underground resistance fighter. After the crew was successfully moved by small boat into Sweden, the Gestapo knocked on this man's door. When he answered, he was shot and killed for his involvement in their escape.

Bob (bottom right) with his crew

Two views of the downed plane, in the field in Denmark. Note the damage to the fuselage, especially in the above photo. They were fortunate to be alive.

Left to Right: Bob Smith, John Smith Sr., John Smith, Jr. And Don Smith (Dad Smith)

In January 1946 we decided to take a few days off and drive our coupe to introduce ourselves to our new in-laws. Jerome, Pennsylvania, the heart of coal mining country, was the home of Bob's parents. I didn't know what to expect, and, of course, they were feeling the same way. Bob was a coal miner before he was drafted in 1942. His family were all coal miners. Bob's dad, John, had been employed in the mine since he was fifteen. This was my introduction to the industry.

When we started driving from Nashville to Pennsylvania I was like a wide-eyed child. Kentucky was so beautiful, white fences and beautiful horses in the huge pastures. Next was Ohio and we began to see snow. In fact there was snow everywhere, no ground to be seen from where we entered Ohio all the way until we reached Bob's home in Jerome and had been there several days. Talk about a winter wonderland...we experienced it! It was beautiful. I had only seen snow once before, when I was in elementary school.

One day while we were there Dad Smith and his three sons were sitting around a wood heater in the dining room. Mother Smith went down the steep, dark stairs into the basement and brought back a heavy bucket of coal. I was flabbergasted that she had not asked one of the men to do that. They didn't move very fast to put the coal in the stove, either. I told Bob to "at least put the coal in the stove!" That was one of the differences in our two families. My mother would never have lifted that heavy item; she would have had one of the sons do it.

After a few days in Pennsylvania we drove to Mississippi, to my parents' home. While there, my elderly paternal aunt Effie died. She had lived with my parents since 1940 when her husband had died.

Bob was very easy-going, so he fit very well into my family. Bob, a tinkerer; was always fixing things for one of my sisters. She would save little fix-it jobs for him every time we visited and he loved doing them. Later at our house in Texas where we lived many years, my daughter told all the neighbor children to bring their broken toys to our house because her daddy was "Mr. Fix It".

In March 1946 Bob was ordered to Wright Patterson Air Force base near Dayton, Ohio. That was the beginning of many moves. The war was over and the occupation of Germany had begun. Bob volunteered to go there, and in July he left. From then until November, when I received my call to join him, I worked in Lewisburg, Tennessee, 55 miles south of Nashville, for Dr. Gordon, a very good surgeon. He was so easy to work for. My duty was to scrub for surgery and assist him. In the afternoon I helped him see office patients; he was a very busy man. One Saturday I remember we saw 90 people. Of course some of them were there only for an injection, blood pressure check, etc. I finally received my port call, telling me exactly when to report to a New York embarkation center, in late November. I visited both of our families, and then traveled by train to New York. The ride was so enjoyable. I wish we could do that now as we did back then; the view of this nation from a train was fantastic.

The voyage from New York to Bremerhaven, Germany, took nine days. We were on an Army transport; all the passengers were dependents, wives and children of military personnel stationed in Germany. The north Atlantic was rough in winter. One night we were singing in the make-shift lounge and suddenly the pump organ someone was playing for us rolled all the way across the floor to the other side of the room.

The occupation of Germany had only recently begun, so they weren't sure where the different units would be sent to work. Our first station was at an air base near a place called Straubing. Germany was so sad; much bomb damage and food was in short supply. Bob was working as a police and prison officer. We lived in the officer barracks and had to walk a couple of blocks to the officer's club for meals. Since we had no furniture Bob had a bed made for us. The wives had nothing to do while our husbands were working, so a friend and I would walk to the gate and catch a ride with troops going to town. It was bitter cold. We walked around the town in the bleak, cloudy, zero degree weather. We were glad to find a Red Cross unit with hot coffee and doughnuts. There weren't many signs of the Christmas season. The stores were not lit with electric lights, they used candles. We didn't see any decorated trees.

We moved to Regensburg, by the Danube River, for only six months. Then we moved to Hamburg. It was one of the cities that were still a disaster area downtown. Rebuilding was amazing in some areas. For instance, in 1946 there were many buildings with bomb damage, however when we returned in 1957, we saw very little bomb damage and a number of new high-rise apartment buildings. Also when we returned to Germany, the Christmas season was much more visible. We saw Christmas trees with candles on them, clamped on the branches where there was no branch right above so as not to start a fire. The candles had a base somewhat like a saucer to catch the wax.

Bob and I went to the library at night along with an Army acquaintance to meet with a very smart lady who helped us learn a little German. She spoke four or five languages. She, like many others in her country, didn't have enough food. After we went home to America we kept in touch and sent her several care packages. When we returned to Germany in 1957 we stopped in Hamburg and visited her.

We were in Germany until June 1947 at which time we received orders to go home. We were being transferred to Mather Air Force Base in California, where Bob was to go to school. I was three months pregnant with our first son, Dale...and what a trip that was! I had so much nausea that I lost nine pounds in nine days. I was in a cabin with a Navy wife, also pregnant. Her husband had heard that if we ate plain soda crackers it would take care of some of the yucky feeling we had. We got very tired of crackers. I was only able to be above deck two times during the nine-day trip.

One of the two times above deck on return voyage in 1947

Summer 1947, Biggs Field, El Paso Texas

The young Bob Smith family

Dale was born at Mather Air Force Base on December 20, 1947. While stationed there, Bob learned aerial and ground radar. He already had expertise as a bombardier on a B-17, so now he could fly as a radar observer and bombardier. He flew lots of hours on a B-29. One night his crew saw a "blip" on the radar scope and Bob realized that it was one of their other planes crash-landing. This experience affected Bob so much that he became psychologically unable to fly.

From Mather we were transferred to Smoky Hill Air Base in Salina, Kansas. While we were in Kansas, Bob had a Temporary assignment in Roswell, New Mexico. While there, we took Dale for treatment for his bowed legs. He was seen by an orthopedist in El Paso who fitted him with braces that he wore them for about six months. From Kansas, we went to Shreveport, Louisiana, and later to Keesler AFB in Biloxi, Mississippi. During the time we lived in Biloxi, our mobile home was parked in a trailer park, near the Red river. One afternoon, I missed Dale and found him heading toward the river. He had gotten out of our area and went through the neighboring park, headed for the river. He was able to move very fast, in spite of the braces.

Bryan, our second son, was born on January 20, 1951, in Biloxi, just three weeks before we left for Fort Meade, Maryland. While stationed there our daughter, Shelley, was born, on June 26, 1955. We were still at Fort Meade when our orders came to go to England in March 1956. By this time our children were eight years, four years, and eight months old. We sailed on the luxury liner *United States*. It was so long that if stood on its end it would be as tall as New York's Empire State building, so we were told. We reached England in only five days. We lived in a hotel for two weeks, then for the next seven months in the small country village of Uffington, where we found a home to rent. Our house was a bake house that was about 300 years old. They had actually baked their bread in the ovens in the back and sold their wares in the front. It was so cold that Shelley had to wear flannel-lined jeans and a shirt inside the house. I attended a huge Church of England there; it had very few worshippers. Our neighbors were very poor. I was a bit embarrassed when the neighborhood children asked to see our refrigerator and I was glad to pay a nice lady to help me around the house.

Shelley had caught a cold while on the ship and could not get rid of it. I took her to a doctor who told me that when she was over the cold we should schedule her for removal of adenoids. We were told if we didn't, she might lose her hearing. On the appointed day, an Air Force man drove us in his pickup to the hospital. It was not the practice at military hospitals for parents to stay with their children, so two nights later he took me back to the hospital to get her. Bob had been worried about how we would get along without her for the two days, since she had not been out of our sight, but we all survived.

My eight-year-old Dale rode the bus to attend an American school. Five-year-old Bryan was able to attend the Church of England school, and I was allowed to visit. It was most interesting. The children were in three class rooms according to age; 7-9 youngest, 9-11 next, and 11-15 the oldest. I was able to help with social functions. One time I took two American-style cakes, one angel food and one marble. Another time I took chocolate and lemon meringue pies. The English folk had never seen any of them before. Also we purchased a globe of the world for the school.

One Saturday Shelley came down with a very high fever. We took her to the dispensary to see the doctor where he ordered ice packs. That's about the hardest thing we ever had to do to a sick child. We did that a number of times during the weekend and by Monday we learned that she had Roseola. The rash was still present but had already cleared up on part of her body.

We lived in Uffington for seven months. During that time, Bryan attended the local school and played with the neighborhood children. En route to school each day, they had to pass the local "sweet" shop (or candy store). One day, the owner of the store called to tell me that Bryan had apparently found a pound note. When I asked what the normal procedure was in that case, he said he would turn it over to the local constable and if no one claimed it, it would be returned to us. Later that day, when I went upstairs, I learned that Bryan had been playing with my British currency (my pound notes) and had taken one to the candy store. I was obliged to call the constable back and let him know the money was actually ours. He came to our home that day after Bryan returned from school and lectured him about taking things that did not belong to him. He sat Bryan in a chair on the kitchen table and talked with him eye to eye, and made a big impression on the youngster about the problems from a life of crime. To this day, I know he remembers his brush with the law.

While we were living in Oxford, we were notified of the accidental death of Ron, a young man from Uffington. I shall never forget the experience of attending the funeral of that 14-year old child who died while mowing the football/cricket field. The village Constable told us the boy had been mowing the field alone and got off to check something. The mower started and rolled over him, rolling him up inside, where he suffocated. When Bob and I reached the village and came to the church, we saw the casket out back sitting on lumber horses. At the start of the funeral, two men carried in the casket on their shoulders and placed it on a stand in front of the Vicar, (Church of England's minister). The service was very short, maybe 15 minutes; nothing was said about the boy, his nature, or even his name. We had known him to be the most community spirited child. The two men returned, moved the casket to the cemetery, and placed it on two wide hemp bands. Then it was carefully lowered to the dirt at the bottom of the deep grave. Everyone approached and looked down into the grave at the brass plate placed on top of the casket. It had Ron's name on it, that was the only way you would know who he was by name, and that you were at the correct funeral. There was no discussion about who he was as an individual or anything about his personality. Ron was the first member of his family to be buried, so he was placed at the bottom of the grave. Other members of his family would be placed on top. It was the saddest funeral I'd ever been to. Afterwards we went to the home of his parents where we were served a very good sandwich, made with slices of homemade bread and salmon from a can, with slices of cucumbers.

Following Uffington, we moved to the outskirts of Oxford, for an additional eight months. We would walk around the area and often saw deer grazing on the grounds of Oxford University. While living in Oxford we took one day and visited London, only 70 miles away. A neighbor kept my baby and I took her seven year old who had never been there. We went to the zoo, saw the Big Ben clock, Buckingham Palace from the outside, the Thames River, Westminster Abbey, and Madame Tussaud's Wax Museum. The figures were amazingly lifelike.

From England we were sent back to Germany. We sailed across the English Channel at night on a ferry, car and all, to Holland. From there we drove to our new station. It was 6:00 p.m. when we arrived, hungry and tired. We went to the snack bar where the juke box was playing Elvis' "All Shook Up." We felt at home.

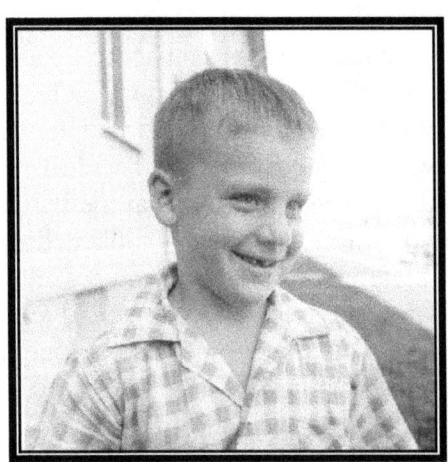

Bryan at Pattonville

I'm not sure how long we actually lived there. Our housing was a huge area near Stuttgart called Pattonville. It had big apartment houses, 18 apartments in each with an American school and a church. Our children were pleased to find other students their age. Both boys received white New Testaments for being present in Sunday school for a whole year. While there, Dale was in cub scouts. During our stay in Pattonville, we also attended the 1958 World's Fair in Brussels, Belgium. There were convenient accommodations available so we were able to spend a week there for little cost. We actually stayed in a tent city, on the outskirts of the park grounds and then took a bus each day. We had food supplies with us and prepared our meals, only having to purchase ice cream and other dessert items. We bought our tickets for the fair right on the grounds of the camping area. We spent five days at the fair for about $75. Shelley was not really old enough to enjoy the fair so she spent much of the time in child care.

Later we moved to the city of Pirmasens, where we stayed until we were ordered home in February 1959. Pirmasens, located in south-east Germany, near the border with France, was the center of the German shoe industry, but during the War, was also an important part of the "Westwall," a series of underground tunnels used to transport military personnel and ammunition. Pirmasens also provided safe accommodation during air raids. After the War the Allies used the lower level as a depot for war material. At this post there were 150 10 to12 year olds. We could not let our children run around in town, there were simply too many of them, so we provided their entertainment which included bowling, parties, cooking, etc. We had to be creative to keep them occupied. One of my activities was cooking classes; the group would select what they wanted to make and bring the ingredients the following week. They would make whatever they had chosen, eat the results and clean up their mess before they were finished. They then would select the project for the next week.

We took one other short trip while in Europe, a trip to Garmisch. At the time, it was a popular spot for recreation for soldiers. We rented a paddle boat for the afternoon, and the boys ended up in a race with local children. I was sitting on the back of the boat during the race, so they blamed their defeat on their "fat momma" on the back of the boat.

Shelley at Pattonville. between 2 & 3 years old

Just before we were to leave for home I needed to pick up a new denture partial at the hospital. I hadn't seen my family in three years and I could not go home wearing a partial that was losing teeth! So I did what was necessary. Our car had been sent on to New York, to be there by the time we arrived. I couldn't drive the neighbor's car because it wouldn't start. I called a taxi, but it never came. So, I walked out to the road which ran past our house and thumbed a ride from a fellow driving a Volkswagen. I knew just enough German to tell him that I needed to get to the hospital and didn't have a car. The man didn't know why I needed to get to the hospital, but he assumed it was important... I've never been driven so fast in my life. The fog was very thick when we left, but by the time I finished at the hospital, the sun was shining and the military buses were running. The day we boarded our ship for home the fog was again very heavy and we could not sail for ten days. Thirteen children were aboard. Needless to say we played lots of games, especially dominoes. I remember the night we finally sailed. We had just finished three full years in Europe. Dale was now eleven, Bryan was eight, and Shelley almost four years old.

Our new station was Fort Bliss at El Paso, Texas. Before going there, we spent some time in Pennsylvania with Bob's family then went to Mississippi. Bob left for Texas while the children and I stayed in Mississippi at my old home until school was over at the end of May. My boys were both in elementary school and rode a bus from Grandma's house to a little town called Pachuta. Bob had been house hunting in El Paso and found one he liked. He bought it and gave me directions on how to get there. We packed the car and I drove all the way from the farm to 9520 Rutledge Place in northeast El Paso with no problems... Bob's directions were so easy to follow. There were no freeways then, so the road was a 2-lane state highway, 1200 miles. Back in the 1950's, very few women traveled alone, much less with three young children.

We were very grateful for the chance to be stationed at El Paso. It is surrounded by mountains, very dry and hot, but since it's a dry heat, there's no humidity. Bob had four years to go before retirement. He was assigned to head a signal unit while at Fort Bliss, not far from our house. The schools were near our home, and very close also was a sign saying "Future Home of Tobin Park Methodist Church." We worked to help build it and attended services there for 20 years.

All three of our children finished their 12 years of public school in El Paso. Bryan was elected as part of the student council in elementary school and he was very active in Boy Scouts. Both Bryan and Dale sang in the high school and church choirs while in their teens. Later, Shelley did the same. The choir teacher, Miss Marjorie Griggs, was fantastic. All my children sang with her and loved and respected her very much. She had the ability to bring out the very best in kids and could instill in them the desire to strive for excellence. At 47 years of age she had a massive stroke and died 24 hours later.

The children thrived in El Paso, being able to be involved in many activities in the community. Bryan was a long time participant in the mountain rescue squad, being ready at a moments notice to go help find lost hikers and climbers. The mountains in the El Paso area are somewhat deceptive in that climbers underestimate the difficulty and often get into trouble up on the mountain and can't get down. He also worked during high school as a delivery person for as donut shop. He would awaken at 0400 and be back in time for school to start at 8:30. One day he came home and told his Dad that his boss needed another driver, so Bob worked there for awhile. Bryan told his Dad that he had recommended him for the job so please do a good job.

Shelley participated in the local Optimist youth group, working at the refreshment stand for the summer ball games, and also sang for many years in town. In 1974, she was part of a 72 voice choir that toured 6 countries in Europe. The funds for the trip were raised through spaghetti dinners, selling newspapers and anything else that would generate money. One of their concerts was in Notre Dame Cathedral in Paris and one of the audience for that concert happened to be a college professor, visiting Paris from the Midwest. He wrote the El Paso newspaper after his trip reporting the concert as superb and commenting that Europeans did not expect the U.S. to export culture, and he was so pleased to hear our group perform.

Dale also performed for many years in El Paso, both in high school and with the UTEP music department. He worked as a blood runner for the El Paso blood bank, responding to calls for blood delivery. This was a job he enjoyed, especially the fast deliveries... he would be asked to meet a sheriff's vehicle to get the blood to outlying areas as quickly as possible. Dale liked to drive fast and didn't mind working on his cars to keep them in good running order. He could replace a transmission in record time and still get to where he needed to be.

Our neighbors were mostly ex-Army. We were very close and I tried to reach out and help them any time I could. I loved to share my specialty, banana bread. One neighbor, who lost her husband in Korea, had five children and they ate lots of what they called my "nana" bread. I still visit El Paso almost every year. I love those folks and the city where we lived for 34 years.

My Banana Bread

1 stick margarine
1 cup sugar
2 eggs
1 ¾ cup all-purpose flour
2 tsp baking powder
½ tsp salt
¼ tsp soda
1 cup mashed ripe bananas
1 tsp vanilla

Cream together the margarine and sugar. Add eggs one at a time, beating well. Sift together the dry ingredients and add.
Add bananas and vanilla. Fill greased pan ½ full.
Bake at 350 degrees until done (usually about an hour). The top will be brown and bread will pull away from the edges of the pan.

Bob retired from the military in 1963; that left him free to pursue an assortment of jobs. He fixed and installed burglar alarms for nine years. He ran an egg farm for three years and we all pitched in to help. We had eight routes a week, delivering eggs directly to individuals' homes. Our children learned to check the eggs, run them through the washing cycle, and grade them according to size, whether small, medium, or large. Bob would go alone out to the farm early each day, and work till early afternoon. Then he would come back into town and wait for the kids to get out of school. Each day for years, at least one of our kids would accompany him back out to the egg farm and pick the eggs, run them through the washing machine etc and return home around 7:00 in the evening. There were also pigs at the farm that were raised for weanlings, (they were sold at about eight weeks old to someone else who raised them for meat). All of the kids had their own pigs that they were responsible for and then received some of the money when the litters were sold.

When Bob retired from the military I went back into nursing part-time for five years. Then I spent two years on full time staff. I worked in a variety of areas at the hospital, including surgery and also the surgical floor. I worked as a nursing supervisor, as well as on call for surgery. I remember once, I was racing to the hospital for a cesarean delivery and was stopped by a police officer, who clocked me at 90 miles per hour. He suggested that if I didn't slow down, I wouldn't get there at all.

I continued working until August 1970, at about the same time I went to an environmental seminar. While there I learned a lot about recycling and the need to preserve our environment. I was so impressed that I decided to become involved and began hauling aluminum cans. I started talking to children in the schools. With permission from the principal, I'd leave a box for the children to bring cans from home; then, I'd go back in a few days and pick them up in my truck. During this can-collecting at several schools, one day I went to pick up the cans at a junior high school and the principal said, "Here comes the lady for her tin cans. She must be the Tin Can Lady." The name stuck. The media heard of it and I am still known in El Paso by that title. I even had my own business cards with my own Tin Can Lady logo. The local high school participated, too, by sponsoring a contest for the students who competed for the honor of their organization being named Club of the Year. Each organization received one point for each can brought to the school. Once I went to the Future Teachers room and picked up 4000 cans. As I remember, the winning club was the French Honor Society.

After a while a neighbor suggested we build a city park; $1400 of the necessary $5000 was raised from children bringing cans from home. The park was on the ground behind Tobin Park Methodist, the church we attended for many years. I approached the trustees of the church to obtain their agreement for the use of the property and then we took it to the city. The final arrangement was that if we would build the park, the city would maintain it on an ongoing basis. The city parks department graded the ground for us and planted the grass, but we did the rest of the work. We actually put in the underground water system, with the help of a local plumber, who gave me two Saturdays of his time and a week of his evenings. When we were ready to plant the trees, the phone company volunteered the time of an employee, who came and dug the holes. We planted 26 trees in about 2 hours with the help of neighborhood residents and children. The playground equipment was purchased with can money and installed by my husband, and other men from the church. It was the most rewarding experience! The park was dedicated on August 10, 1973.

I was invited by the Coors Brewing Company in Golden, Colorado, to visit their facility for a VIP tour of their recycling process. I was also appointed by my alderman to serve on the Sanitation Advisory Board for four years. My involvement in environmental activities grew and in 1980 I was chosen as First Lady of Beta Sigma Phi. A luncheon was held in my honor January 1981 at the El Paso Country Club. I'm still amused when I think of 250 women coming to a luncheon to hear El Paso's Tin Can Lady.

The business card Bob had made for me

One day Bryan came home and told his Dad that he knew of an MG sports car for sale. Bob checked it out and bought it. That was the start of a 20-year hobby. Bob loved to drive, but he also loved to work on cars. He had this friend at a local junk yard, (Wimpy) and they became buddies. Bob visited regularly to check on MG parts, and Wimpy would trade him MG parts for rebuilding starters and other work. He had a sweet tooth so Bob was also able to get some his MG parts for banana bread. Eventually Bob had enough parts to not only completely restore the first MG, but he could have probably built several more. He did restore a second car that he sold to our neighbor. During his retirement we took a number of trips by car: enough that I have now been in 40 of the 48 contiguous states. That travel reinforces for me the beauty and unique freedoms of our country.

Dale graduated from Irvin High School in 1965, Bryan in 1969, and Shelley in 1973. Dale attended the University of Texas at El Paso (UTEP) for several years then went to Phoenix and took courses in computer science. While living in Phoenix, he stayed with Bob's aunt Pauline. She had lived in the Phoenix area since the 30's and loved having the company. In fact Dale and Mischa both stayed with her until he completed his training program, about six months after their wedding.

At age 23, Dale married Patricia Yanez (known to the family as Mischa), on August 1, 1970, in El Paso. Dale began working for Otis Elevators in 1971 and has continued to work with elevators for more than thirty years. He is the most experienced in the area. He seems to have his fathers' talent for working with his hands and with electrical things. Mischa completed her college education and was certified as a teacher. She worked in the El Paso school system for a few years, and currently works doing bookkeeping.. They have one son, Robert, who is now 16 years old and still live in the El Paso area.

Dale with young son, Robert

Dale and Mischa, at First Lady Day

Bryan joined the Army in November 1969, and because he was such an avid reader and had high entrance test scores, he was offered an appointment to the US Military Academy at West Point. First he had to attend nine months of rigorous prep school to supplement his math and science skills.

Bob giving Bryan his oath at graduation.

Bryan successfully completed prep school and graduated from the Academy in 1975; we were all proud of him. His father was delighted to be able to give him his oath when Bryan was commissioned as a Second Lieutenant, upon graduation. He served in a variety of stations while on active duty, one of them in Germany, where he met his wife. Lisa Evans, was visiting her older brother, Mike, also in the military, and stationed in Germany, when she went roller skating one evening and met Bryan. The rest, as they say, is history. They were married in March of 1979 in Bayard West Virginia, after Bryan completed his tour in Germany. Besides Germany, Bryan was on active duty in Texas, North Carolina, and Kansas.

He left active duty in 1988, and began a second career with the automotive industry, first working for Ford, now for Visteon, a company who makes component parts. He stayed in the military as a reservist however and completed a total of more than thirty years of service before retiring as a Colonel in 2005. In 2003, Bryans' reserve unit was activated and he spent nine months as part of a logistical team in Europe, in conjunction with the liberation of Iraq. While in Europe, he took a weekend to go to Copenhagen, hoping to find the spot where his father's B-17 had crashed in 1944.. He didn't succeed, but did find the Memorial Garden where the man is buried who hid the crew in his apartment, later being shot by the Gestapo for his assistance. Bryan was able to put flowers on the grave, and saluted the man. A passerby took his picture, which I now have. It is especially touching to me since this man saved his father's life.

Bryan at grave in Copenhagen, Memorial Grounds in honor of resistance fighters

Lisa is a paraprofessional in the local school system and works as a teachers' assistant. Bryan and Lisa now live in Michigan and have three children, Andrew, 25, Patrick, 23, and Abby, 21 years old.

At Abby's high school graduation, Andrew, Mildred, Abby, and Patrick

Bob with Abby

Bryan and Lisa's wedding, March 1979

Shelley graduated in 1973 and attended the local college for two years. She transferred to Texas Woman's University where she studied nursing and received her Bachelor of Science. During college, she taught in child care centers, both in El Paso and in Houston. Later, she went to Arizona State University where she received her Masters degree in Nursing of Children. Shelley worked in Forth Worth, Texas, shortly after receiving her MS degree. She worked with an x-ray technician named Roberta Wieting. One weekend she accompanied Roberta to Oklahoma. After arriving there, they had an accident. Mike Wieting, Roberta's son, came to get his mother, and that's where he and Shelley met. They married in March 1985 in Oklahoma City. Mike is now an osteopathic physician and specialist in physical medicine and rehabilitation. He is a professor at the Michigan State University College of Osteopathic Medicine. Shelley is the past national president of the Advocates for the American Osteopathic Association. She is a registered nurse but is not working because her job as president of this organization required much travel and time.

Shelley, hiking in the mountains of El Paso

Shelley with Mike

My husband had a wonderful sense of humor, he was very good-natured and friendly to all. Bob was very proud of me and always helped me in whatever I was involved in. He drove our truck to pick up tin cans. He accompanied me on my numerous trips. Because he had retired from the military at an early age and then completely at age 62, we had many years to travel and do things together before his health started to fail. I preferred to travel by car instead of flying so Bob would bring the needed tools for whatever project was scheduled when we visited our children's homes. All three of our children are good with their hands and are able to make things... skills they undoubtedly got from their father.

Bob had developed diabetes in his 50's, which eventually caused other health problems. Cardiac problems started early in 1990 and he was hospitalized multiple times between November 1990 and July 1991. He had several problems as a result of the diabetes which eventually resulted in his death. He died on July 11, 1991, and was buried in the military cemetery at Fort Bliss, El Paso, Texas. Our son-in-law, Mike Wieting, wrote a tribute to Bob shortly after his death. He said in part:

> "In 1991 the Smith family lost a beloved husband, father, grandfather, brother, and uncle who had a profound effect upon many lives by just being himself and teaching those around him by word and deed. Bob Smith was a shining example of human decency whose disarming smile and kind, unassuming, gentle ways were contagious. Bob never met a stranger and always gave freely of himself to others. By doing so, he showed others that all people merit attention and respect, have worth, and that basic human kindness is the foundation upon which we should build. Bob was a man of many talents; a mechanical wizard, he could fix virtually anything and was quickly able to figure out the most puzzling problem. While working his mechanical magic, diagnosing the latest automotive disease, or repairing some electrical device, he demonstrated the importance of systematic problem solving and the pride taken in doing a job really well.
>
> Bob showed us that skills are helped along by some natural talent and intelligence, but are largely due to hard work, self-motivated pursuit of one's goals and setting standards of excellence.
>
> A voracious reader and life-long learner, always interested in learning something new or doing it better, he showed us the value of intellect, and that diligent attention to a task would bring it to a satisfactory completion.

Bob was an excellent example of a spouse and parent; his devotion to his family was always unquestionable and they always came first. He was a loyal, loving husband, showing that a successful marriage is a joint partnership based on love, cooperation, support of individual and common goals, not material things, politically expedient behavior or keeping up with what others are doing. He showed by example that the best way to parent was to spend time with children, yet let them go their own way with supportive advice and guidance, to be genuinely interested in them as people and in their pursuits and to be dependable, responsible, self-reliant, honest, hard working individuals who take pride in what they do.

Bob lives on in many ways. Each of his family has their own special memories of him, but memories aren't the only way Bob is still with us. All we have to do is look at his wife, widely known for her community service, preceded by her professional nursing career and three multitalented children who are professionally successful, happily married, and with unlimited potential for achievement in life."

About eighteen months after Bob's passing, I felt called to make a difference in the lives of children. El Paso, though, is a large city with 14 high schools. I didn't think I could go to all of those schools. So I decided to sell my house and move back to the farm in Mississippi. Shelley and I bought three acres of the original homestead, including my brother's house, where I now live. While I loved El Paso, it felt good to be back home.

Bob on visit to Shelley's, mid 80's

Bob with grandson Robert, December 1990

Chapter 5
A Second Calling

Back when the races were more separated, we went to black churches only when they were having revivals, usually in the fall. When I first moved back home in 1993 I was invited to attend some black churches. In fact, I taught Sunday school in a local black church for almost two and a half years. Some of these people I had known when I was growing up and we worked on the farm together and we'd been friends ever since. But I sensed some opposition to my attending and working in the black church; some from family members, some from people in the community and some from the congregation. This hasn't been much of an issue though as I have had the pleasure of helping with several different Bible Schools at two churches and have also been able to share one of the craft projects that I make with kids at these same churches.

Other activities that have kept me busy since my return to Mississippi involve the artesian well on highway 512. Years ago people came to this county and were drilling for oil. One of the test sites was along the current highway. No oil was found but it has been flowing with water for as long as I can remember. One day as I passed the well, on the way to town, I saw an elderly lady squatting by the well, trying to fill a gallon jug with a cup. The well had been vandalized and the pipe was lying on the ground, making it very difficult to get the water. I decided right then that I would find a well digger and get it repaired. I was able to locate someone and we set a date to meet at the well, so that he could tell me what repairs could be done and what they would cost. This man gave me the approximate cost for the repair and I also learned that he was the son of one of my high school classmates, class of 1940. He fixed the well by adding galvanized pipe to force the water to form a stream as it comes out of the ground. Another local gentleman contributed a metal grate, which allows people to set their water jug on something when it is filling. When Hurricane Katrina hit this area last August, it was very fortunate that this source of water was available, since the pumping mechanisms for the county were not functional for quite some time. Many in the community were very happy that the well was working and providing a convenient source of fresh drinking water.

Since approximately 1994, a year after my return to Mississippi, I have also been working two days a week at a local nursing home, as a volunteer, doing finger nails for the residents. This has been an activity that both the residents and I enjoy. They sit for many hours in the lobby and stare across at one another because they have little to occupy their time... visiting with me and watching me do the nails for their fellow residents gives them something else to do. They seem to enjoy it and it is something I have been pleased to provide. As a registered nurse, I am very capable of doing nails, while also being careful to watch for indications of circulatory problems etc.

In the summer of 1996 I called on the Superintendent of Education and received permission to address the students in the local high school. Since then I've had the pleasure of addressing all of the 9th grade health classes. The students are most attentive and seem quite interested in what I talk about with them. This is especially unique in that there is almost 70 years between our ages. I open this talk by giving the students some of our Christian heritage, in the form of quotes from Christopher Columbus, John Adams, and George Washington. We also discuss the Declaration of Independence. From there we delve deeply, from my Christian perspective, into the subjects of abortion, sexually transmitted diseases, pornography, and homo-sexuality. No question is off-limits. I do wonder sometimes if they are as interested in what I have to say as they seem to be that at 84 years old I am still driving myself to get there.

Since Bob and I married just five days following the end of World War II. I've collected lots of items, beginning with the picture of the downed B-17 Bob and his crew crashed into the Denmark field. Occasionally I have the opportunity to present what I have and know about the war to 10th grade history classes.

I have good rapport with youth and thank God for that. I've helped with several Bible schools; which are a week of study, crafts, music, etc. One day I went to the director of a local child care center, with an idea that some children may have limited interaction with people of a different race, and that by having that experience they may be better prepared to interact when they get to kindergarten or first grade and have teachers and classmates of other races. For one whole year, when I could be there, I have read to these children, who sit on the floor while I hold the book so that they can see the pictures as I read. They then stand up and come to my open arms until all 25 of them get a hug. It's a marvelous experience…I love it. Recently I went to a graduation of five who are ready for kindergarten. My goal is to make it easier for these children to learn in the public school system and thus have a better life.
All this is such a joy to me because I consider my return to Mississippi as a call from the Holy Spirit: a Divine Mandate to make a difference in the lives of the children. With His help, I will. These projects and activities give me a mechanism to contribute and by doing so, I am fulfilling what I believe to be my calling. It does not matter whether others agree or not, this is what I must do. I am firm in my beliefs. And I'm not shy about sharing them. In one of my recent letters to the editor of a local newspaper I wrote:

"All we have was made and given to us by the Creator God. He gave us rules and laws to live by and He loved us so much He gave His son to die for our sins. We are to love God first then love our neighbors as ourselves."

Me in Canada, 2004

My trusty steed at the Toronto Zoo

Epilogue:

For some time, I've felt that I wanted to write down everything I could remember of my life and even some that was told to me at an early age. I have tried to do that here.

I've had a wonderful life... I've enjoyed all of it; from the cotton patch to the operating room to overseas with my military husband of almost 46 years.

I just wanted to share it with you.

Enjoy!

Mildred Price Smith

*Map of Germany
Pirmasens, Stuttgart, Regensburg and Straubing:
places we lived while stationed overseas.*

Appendix

Assorted Photos

Dale, Mischa and Robert

Bailey and Nella Price, approximately 1960

Building the Park & Grading the Land in El Paso

Building the Park, Digging trenches for Water Lines

The Park in El Paso Today (2005)

The Park Today with New Playground Equipment

Me and My Kids, Passport Photo 1956

Me with Kids in Germany ~ 1958

Trailer in Salina Kansas

Family Portrait ~ 1956

Bob with Lady in Regensburg – 1946

Doug and Maybelle – 2002

Me and Kathleen – 2002

Me and my grandson, Robert (December 2005)

www.ingramcontent.com/pod-product-compliance
Lightning Source LLC
Chambersburg PA
CBHW070321100426
42743CB00011B/2502